Margaret Hillenbrand

BRITAIN IN PICTURES
THE BRITISH PEOPLE IN PICTURES

LIFE AMONG THE SCOTS

GENERAL EDITOR
W. J. TURNER

The Editor is most grateful to all those who have
so kindly helped in the selection of illustrations
especially to officials of the various public
Museums Libraries and Galleries and
to all others who have generously
allowed pictures and MSS
to be reproduced

LIFE AMONG THE SCOTS

JANET ADAM SMITH

WITH
8 PLATES IN COLOUR
AND
21 ILLUSTRATIONS IN
BLACK & WHITE

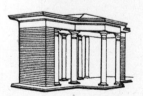

COLLINS · 14 ST. JAMES'S PLACE · LONDON
MCMXXXXVI

PRODUCED BY
ADPRINT LIMITED LONDON

PRINTED IN GREAT BRITAIN BY
CLARKE & SHERWELL LTD NORTHAMPTON
ON MELLOTEX BOOK PAPER MADE BY
TULLIS RUSSELL & CO LTD MARKINCH SCOTLAND

LIST OF ILLUSTRATIONS

PLATES IN COLOUR

THE CITY OF EDINBURGH
Coloured lithograph by I. Clark, published 1824

MARKET STREET, ABERDEEN
Coloured lithograph after A. Simpson and P. C. Auld

THE PENNY WEDDING
Water colour sketch by Sir David Wilkie, 1785-1841

HIGHLAND CHIEFS IN THE STEWART AND GORDON TARTANS
Coloured engraving after J. Logan by R. Havell, Junr. from Logan's *The Scottish Gael*, 1831

FLORA MACDONALD
Oil painting by Allan Ramsay, c. 1749

THE EMIGRANTS
Oil painting by William McTaggart, 1891

THE KIRK, ISLE OF WITHORN, SCOTLAND
Water colour by Sir Muirhead Bone

THE CLYDE FROM PORT GLASGOW
Oil painting by Stanley Spencer

BLACK AND WHITE ILLUSTRATIONS

PICTISH HORSEMEN
Carving on the back of a stone cross found at St. Madoes in the Carse of Gowrie

BEFORE THE REFORMATION

AS soon as a traveller from the South arrives in Scotland he finds himself among people whose language, customs and outlook are not exactly those of the comparable class in England. He finds too that, unlike the English, who assume that the way they do a thing is the only reasonable way to do it, the Scots are conscious of such differences, and ready to argue about them. Salt in the porridge, for instance : the stranger (who would prefer sugar) quickly learns not only that taking salt is the proper Scots way, but that this is an issue in which the Scot has invested some emotion and national pride. Few, indeed, of the differences from life in England can be dismissed as purely matters of taste. They are nearly all rooted in history—and geography—and if the stranger is to appreciate fully the quality of life among the Scots he must begin by

7

looking backward. Our love of argument owes something to the Reformation ; our touchiness at hearing 'English' for 'British' to the Union of Parliaments ; our fierce patriotism at Hampden Park and Murrayfield has in it memories of Bannockburn and Flodden ; and salt in the porridge is a daily reminder that Scotland has always been a hard country, where it was unwise to cultivate luxurious habits.

"What could have brought us hither ?" cried the French knights who had landed in Scotland in 1385 to march against the common enemy ; "We have never known till now what was meant by poverty and hard living." Here is one main thread in the pattern of life among the Scots. Look at a map : more than three-quarters of the country over six hundred feet high ; the lower straths separated by mountain barriers ; the coast fretted and indented. In a poorer soil, and a colder, wetter climate, the harvest could never be so certain as in England. Even our biggest towns are more exposed to the forces of nature, as any stranger to Edinburgh bitterly realises when his hat is torn off by gusts skirling up the hill into George Street from off the Forth. And to the hard living dictated by geography, history added another ; for throughout the wars of independence it was the fertile part of the country, the Lothians and the valley of the Tweed, that was raided and harried by the enemy from the South.

So it is not surprising that the fine arts of civilisation came late to Scotland. The Romans had come, but not as civilisers, only as military raiders and outposts ; there was no *pax Romana* in Scotland. Civilisation began to creep in later, a little with St. Ninian to Galloway, a little with St. Columba to the West. Among the earliest conscious civilisers were the eleventh-century Malcolm Canmore and his English queen Margaret. They brought in southern manners and language, they gave power and land to Norman knights. Margaret has been credited with inventing tartans ; but she called her sons by English names, discouraged Gaelic, and frowned on the Celtic Church. Stitching copes, chasubles and altar-cloths with 'certain women of noble birth,' she was perhaps the first to make the Scot feel provincial.

Regarded from the standpoint of London or Paris, life among the Scots, to those French knights in 1385, must certainly have looked provincial. But that has never been the right way to look at Scotland. In working out her way of life she has drawn largely from other cultures ; but she has had to make her borrowings work in terms of her own situation. If some of the institutions of Western Europe looked a little transformed by the time they reached Scotland, that was a condition of their survival there at all. Feudalism, for instance, came to Scotland with the Norman knights ; but there was never so large a servile class as in England or France. There, in the manors of the wide and sheltered lowlands, was a place for men tied to the land ; in Scotland the primary need was for men to reclaim mountain, marsh and forest, and to drive out the invader, whether of the nation,

8

JAMES EARL OF DOUGLAS WINS SIR HENRY PERCY'S PENNON
DURING THE FIGHT BEFORE NEWCASTLE, 1388
Illumination by Philippe de Mazerolles, c. 1456, from the Chronicles of Froissart

family or clan. And though a Greek traveller from Venice complained that Scotland lacked the vine, the olive and the fig-tree, and a doctor called in from Italy in 1552 was surprised that the Archbishop of St. Andrews

9

had no clock, nearly all foreigners were impressed by the independence of the common people. The ways of life imposed by the country, and the ways introduced from abroad—life among the Scots can be read as a story of the stresses between these two forces. Has it flourished most when they have been most nearly balanced ? We can at any rate look and see ; and perhaps start by noting that the two great nationalist poems of Scotland's independence, Blind Harry's *Wallace* and Barbour's *Bruce*, were completely within the Anglo-French medieval tradition.

Some early records show us Scotland in its aspect of a Western European State. There are the monasteries established by the same great Orders that built in Italy, France, England and Spain, and most of the houses are closely linked with England—Dunfermline founded by monks from Canterbury, Scone from Pontefract, Paisley from Wenlock. There is the pattern of Western Christendom, and the rhythm of the feasts and observances of the Christian year. When we read of the traditional Candlemas play of the Aberdeen craftsmen—with the smiths providing the Three Kings of Cologne, the Dyers the Emperor, the Masons the Three Knights, and the Tailors Our Lady, St. Bride and St. Helen—then we see Scotland directly linked with every other place where the Three Kings were being played. But when we read John Major on the Feast of the Nativity, commonly celebrated "in a tavern not in a church, in such intemperance of eating and drinking as is the enemy of chastity, in dances and lewd songs"—we are rather reminded of the distance of Scotland from Rome.

When the French champion, Messire de Lalain, having met and conquered the flower of knights of France, Spain and Portugal, sent a herald to Scotland in 1448 to challenge James Douglas, and when he later did meet him, and beat him with lance, axe, sword and dagger—he was acknowledging Scottish chivalry as comparable with that of France : but his countryman Froissart was far more conscious of the differences between the Scottish fighting-man and the French or English. Almost with awe, he noted the simplicity and economy of their arrangements—no transport, no provisions, no wine, only a bag of meal at the saddle-bow and a metal plate to cook it on. Scotland was the country to which Ferdinand and Isabella sent an ambassador to find a husband for their daughter ; it was also the country about which no tale was too tall to be believed, where barnacles fell off trees into the water and hatched out geese, where volcanoes abounded, and strange floating islands.

There are no Scottish Pastons of the fourteenth century to give us, through their letters, a detailed picture of everyday life as it appeared to the people living it. But from various records we can imagine some of the main lines, in the last hundred years before the Reformation made a break in the pattern. Highest in standard of living came the monasteries which, with about half the wealth of the country in their hands, could afford more comfort than the nobles, and most of the rich furnishings and luxuries

AENEAS SILVIUS PICCOLOMINI AT THE COURT OF JAMES I OF SCOTLAND
Fresco painted in 1503 by Bernardino Pintoricchio in the Cathedral Library, Siena

sent to Scotland in the fifteenth century by the Scots agent at Middelburg went to ecclesiastics. They were the main source of the few books available; they cultivated the arts of building and carving (though many of the craftsmen were imported from England) ; they made some attempt to spread education. Their standard was matched only by the richer town burgesses. Unlike the nobleman with his castle and retinue to keep up, the burgess could consider only his own family and his own domestic needs ; and he had more ready money. So while he could afford silk furnishings from abroad, the nobleman had to make shift with skins from the wolves which were still plentiful in Scotland.

For the nobles, as for the peasants living in small turf huts, there had been for generations little security from the violence of wars with the English and feuds within their own country. And yet, by the time of James IV (1488-1513) there was a surprising amount of energy left over from the hard business of merely living. The poets give evidence here. Dunbar's *Two Married Women and the Widow* can gossip of lovers, deceived husbands, lawn kerchiefs, jewelled rings, furred gowns, and the chances of gallantry at plays, preachings and pilgrimages, with never a word of wars, feuds, or the street fights that were common in the cities. Insecurity is indeed never far off from Dunbar's world—"All erdly joy returns in pain" —but it also holds songs, ballads and plays, dancings at court, and it is peopled by doctors and philosophers, astrologers, artists and orators, musicians and minstrels, as well as by men of arms and tillers of the soil. And learning did not wait for wealth or assured peace ; already there were Universities at St. Andrews, Glasgow and Aberdeen.

During this reign of James IV, indeed, the stamp of Europe was firmly set, not so much on Scottish society as a whole, as on the Scottish court. Foreign visitors, who expected to find a half-barbarous country, were impressed by the king who spoke Latin, French, German, Italian and Spanish, who was interested in science, medicine and theology (though without much taste for art and letters), and by his natural son, the young Archbishop of St. Andrews, who had been taught by Erasmus in France. And yet, even at the Court, it was Europe with a Scots accent. Already we can see certain characteristics that are usually credited to Calvinism. There is the Scottish Sunday, and James refusing to ride for any consideration, not even to Mass (half a century later Mary suppressed the playing of Robin Hood and Little John on Sundays). There is the concentration on results, the suspicion of pleasure for pleasure's sake ; James ordained that whereas shooting and archery be practised, and wapinschaws held four times in the year, there should be no "foot-ball, golf, or other such unprofitable sports." There is the Scottish censoriousness : James, reports the Spanish Ambassador, has given up his love-making, not only "from fear of God, but also from fear of scandal in this world, which is thought very much of here."

12

JOHN KNOX PREACHING BEFORE THE LORDS OF THE CONGREGATION
Detail from a sketch by Sir David Wilkie, 1821

AFTER THE REFORMATION

ALTHOUGH the Reformation may be held accountable for a certain austerity and lack of grace in Scottish life, yet during the years that the Reformers were at their work, life in Scotland was in a material sense becoming much easier. The money that had gone to Rome now stayed in the country. With artillery able to dent any castle wall, merchants and gentlemen building new houses were free to think of comfort more than defence. Instead of dining at a narrow board fifteen feet long, the company sat in a circle round a table. Easy chairs and cushions

13

began to replace benches and settles ; carpets and rugs, the covering of bent grass. Books appeared, and painted pictures. Dessert was introduced in the best houses, before it was adopted in London ; the table was cleared, fruit and sweets were served in another room. This pleasant custom came from France ; to the Auld Alliance between the countries was due much of the gentler side of Scottish life, including the national taste for claret based on the trade with Bordeaux and Rochelle. The young men of family who went abroad to study philosophy at Leyden, law at Utrecht, medicine in Paris, or who fought as soldiers of fortune in Sweden, Germany and Holland, helped to introduce new dishes, new drinks, and new manners : it was a well-travelled aristocracy, not yet looking to London as example and hall-mark.

Town life became steadily more civilised through the seventeenth century. Earlier travellers to Edinburgh had, to a man, been impressed chiefly by the method of throwing out refuse when, to a cry of "Gardyloo !" the housewife six stories up in one of the lands of the High Street, would empty her slops out of the window. (And few observers were as charitable as Defoe, who thought that if London or Bristol had as high and crowded buildings, and as little water, they would have rivalled Edinburgh in dirt). But the Englishmen who came north with Cromwell's army, or made tours for pleasure later in the century, were able to notice too how solid the houses were, how well paved the streets. Glasgow, though, was the favourite town : "fair, large, and well-built, cross-wise, somewhat like unto Oxford, the streets very broad and pleasant," its charming college-grounds with their orchard, its well-dressed people, its enterprising merchants.

Life was in general more comfortable, but not most people's view of life. To the medieval Scot, the world had a traditional pattern in which he took his place. But the new religion threw a terrifying burden on the individual. He had won his independence by using his own judgment ; now there were no limits to what he must judge. However sanctioned by custom or time, every action must now be questioned ; and, questioned in the fierce light of Heaven or Hell, anything that spoke merely of pleasure had no chance at all. The old outlook had sanctified the necessary actions of daily life ; the dominant philosophy regarded life as at the best a vexatious delay in attaining salvation, at the worst a continuous wrestle with the devil in all his forms. So to the rigid Presbyterian, any increase of material comfort was a trifling with eternity ; and cooking, which under French influence had begun to be an art in Scotland, was once more a mere physical necessity. The reasoning of the earlier Reformers had been directed at first principles, and they let minor points of behaviour look after themselves —Knox played bowls on Sunday, James Melville was brought up to fence, golf, swim and practise archery. But half a century later there was nothing that escaped the eye of the fervid Presbyterian. The General Assembly in 1650 forbade mixed dancing of any kind ; people who played cards and

MODERN MODERATION STRIKINGLY DISPLAYED

Dismiss; I order every one of you, go home and desire your Parents to teach you I have a right to be heard I say go Home—

Sir some of them have no Parents

'THE SUNDAY SCHOOL VIEWED WITH SUSPICION BY THE CHURCH OF SCOTLAND'
Etching by John Kay, 1799

travelled on Sunday were held to be fully as bad as those who bow to the altar, or wear cope and rotchett. Nor was there a Court to balance the Assembly's social influence, or withstand its intrusion.

In the old days Scotland had enjoyed a fine crop of festivals, the Christian, the Norse, the Celtic—Scottish quarter days still follow the

15

Celtic division of the year. Now the Christian feasts also came under suspicion: Christmas had often been kept ill, but the Kirk made it a duty not to keep it at all. Christian feasts had incorporated and sanctified pre-Christian rites, as Christmas did Yule. Now, forbidden Christmas, the Scot put all his energies into the entirely secular pleasures of Hogmanay (or New Year's Eve), and the link between his religion and his merry-making was snapped. The red-letter days in the Presbyterian's year were the Communion Sundays. The sacrament was usually celebrated in each parish once a year ; preceded by a service of preparation, followed by a thanksgiving, and regarded with awful solemnity. Part of the feeling in which it was held came from the circumstances of its celebration by the Covenanters in the years when they were persecuted. Received on an open hillside, with sentries posted and the congregation risking their lives, the Communion had seemed doubly awful and precious.

Some of this awe was extended to the minister. Visitors from England noted that here the minister was held in far greater esteem, and something of this feeling still persists. "The ministry" has been an ambition to set before any promising boy ; never, as sometimes in England, a consolation prize to a younger son. Nor has this attitude been affected by the hope of obtaining a plum. There are no plums in the Church of Scotland.

> Make me, O Sphere-descended Queen,
> A Bishop, or at least a Dean—

wrote an ambitious young Wykehamist. But however the Scottish student venerated Learning, all the dignity that he could aspire to would be to serve as Moderator—for one year only. The comedies of Barchester have no Scottish equivalent.

The Reformation bestowed one major pleasure on the Scot—a taste for religious argument and controversy. James VI bullied an unwilling Jesuit into a debate that lasted for five hours ; Sir John Lauder, arriving in Paris to complete his education in 1665, accosted the curé after Mass and disputed with him for an hour, in Latin, on Purgatory and Predestination. This taste, together with the conviction that religion was really the most important thing in a man's life, resulted in the schisms and disruptions that have so marked the history of the Church in Scotland. Another by-product of the national absorption in religion, and the rigid individualism of the Presbyterian approach, was a sense of easy familiarity with God—and with the Devil. Hell was a familiar concept to every medieval church-goer, and the fear of hell had been played upon long before Calvin. But the Scot of the seventeenth century had a particularly keen sense of the evil stalking through the world beside him ; and perhaps the only way to make the concept bearable was to see it as something homely as well as grim, familiar as well as dreadful. Johnston of Warriston gives practical instructions to gentlemen of Galloway "to resist the devil and maik him

16

THE CITY OF EDINBURGH

Coloured lithograph by I. Clark, published 1824

By courtesy of the Parker Gallery, London

MARKET STREET, ABERDEEN

Coloured lithograph after A. Simpson and P. C. Auld

flye way lyk a dog with his tayle between his legges." Burns himself underlines a national difference when he puts Milton's dignified lines about a dignified Satan—

O Prince! O Chief of many thronèd pow'rs,
That led th'embattled Seraphim to war!

at the head of his own 'Address to the Deil.' *His* Deil is Auld Hornie, Nick or Clootie, Auld Hangie, Cloots, or Nickie-Ben—and the Scots diminutive *ie* usually denotes affection.

To be on easy terms with God was a Presbyterian tradition that has lasted to our own day, encouraged by the Presbyterian emphasis on extempore prayer. "Oh Lord, we thank Thee for thy bounteous harvest," prayed one such minister, within living memory, before his Aberdonian congregation, "The earth has brought forth an hundred fold, nay, a thousand fold. All the land is covered with Thy golden bounty—" and here his tone became more practical than lofty, "with the exception of a few bare patches round about Stonehaven scarcely worth mentioning, Oh Lord."

In the view of the extremists, the Presbyterian discipline (which was little concerned with men's working lives) scrutinised every pleasure and amusement with a jealous eye ; but though ministers might deplore the slackness of "the younger set" in religious observance, they could not altogether change people's tastes and natures. A dromedary and a baboon, shown in Edinburgh in 1656 at threepence a time, made much profit for their keeper ; a few years later a team of acrobats and actors performed in the Canongate to large crowds. An Edinburgh lawyer of the time paid a shilling for seeing a lioness at Kirkaldy, and three shillings to go to the races.

Lord Wemyss, who lived all through the wars of religion, had little to say about them in his diary : his interests were in his coal-mines and salt-pans, the new walls on his estate, the chartering of a ship for London, the proposed additions to his house. The nobility as a whole, sound Covenanters and all, did not allow themselves to be unduly irked by the Presbyterian view of life. Ministers like Robert Baillie would not scruple to denounce the highly born who were slack in going to church, and possibly this sort of friction was a factor in turning the aristocracy's eyes towards England : by the end of the century the movement had become, in one observer's opinion, "a prodigious run." Noblemen began to spend winters in the South ; to have their children educated there ; and after the Union of Parliaments in 1707, a Scotsman could cry bitterly that "the greatest estates in Scotland, in land-rent, are all taken to England in specie ; Buccleugh, Roxburgh, Argyle, Montrose, etc." The aristocracy, cosmopolitan in taste and outlook at the end of the sixteenth century, by the end of the seventeenth was on the high road to being anglicised.

17

EIGHTEENTH CENTURY

AFTER 1707, Scotland had neither King nor Parliament; there was a blank at the heart of the country. Edinburgh no longer drew to itself the 145 noblemen and 160 commoners of the old Parliament, nor was their loss offset by closer and stimulating contact with the other capital. In Queen Anne's day the London mailbag sometimes brought only one letter to Edinburgh, there was no regular service of coaches. Nor was there much coming and going between different parts of the country; but those who did have to make journeys supplied one of the diversions of the gentry's life. Most travellers counted on putting up at private houses; with the result that the inns were merely ale-houses, in great contrast to those of England. Very different pictures of accommodation in Scotland are given according to whether the traveller stayed mostly in houses, like Johnson and Faujas de St. Fond, or at inns, like the Wordsworths and Keats. The private house of the eighteenth century might lack carpets, dinner might be eaten in the bedroom, and off wooden platters, the guest might have to double up with a stranger in a box-bed—but he would have a warm welcome, plentiful broth and mutton, haggis and cock-a-leekie, the endless hens that were part of a tenant's rent to the laird, and the admirable claret. Always forced to be careful of his cash (£100 a year was a usual income for a landowner, £500 marked him as rich) the laird was generous of his kind. As the century went on, agricultural improvements became a dominant interest of the country gentry, to the benefit of their rent-roll and their table (which now saw fresh meat in winter, turnips, carrots, onions and potatoes as well as the immemorial kale)—if not of their general culture. For when Ambassador Keith came home from Vienna and Petersburg in 1764, he complained that the lairds' sons were no longer sent abroad to enlarge their minds or improve their manners, and could now talk of nothing but dung and bullocks.

With little to bring the regions together, each fostered a vigorous and characteristic local life. There was, for instance, the life of the fishermen up and down the east coast : independent, hardy and superstitious people, fearing to meet a minister on the way to the boat, or to speak of a salmon; the men, masters of the sea, the women, selling the fish and controlling the money. They kept themselves distinct from their farming neighbours inland; and to this day the Newhaven or Musselburgh fishwife who, with her creel of herring and haddock may be met on a bus going out to sell and chaffer in Pentland villages, strikes a bold and exotic note among the other passengers.

There was the life of the Borders; though this was not all of one piece. The richer soil of the Eastern Marches won over its inhabitants to the peaceful arts of agriculture, but in the hills of the Middle and Western Marches, the tradition of the Border raid and foray had by no means died

LIBBERTON WYND, EDINBURGH
Etching by Walter Geikie, 1795-1837

out. In the long wars against England, Borderers had grown out of the way of raising crops for the enemy to reap : cattle were better, but cattle too could be captured. And long after the wars were over, the cattle-lifting went on, both sides of the Border, with a regular system of reprisals which both sides acknowledged. If the cows stolen by one Englishman were not

19

recovered another must lose his. These methods blurred the distinction between just reprisal and plain stealing ; and they ensured for the Border reiver the kind of regard we give to the jockey or the footballer. (The modern Borderer lifts, not cattle, but salmon ; poaching is a general sport. There was trouble this war with a Border battalion in the Highlands ; the river was in spate, the salmon were running, and every man was out in the water with bayonets, camouflage nets and hand grenades, to the shock of the more law-abiding natives). Fighting was in the Borderer's blood ; and when circumstances limited his opportunities, his pugnacity found new outlets. Borderers, if we can believe Scott, have more than their fair share of the Scot's love of litigation : Dandie Dinmont's pride and dignity demanded that he should embark on a long and complicated lawsuit with Jock o' Dawston Cleugh about a parcel of bare land that might feed two hogs in a good year; and certainly it was a real Lowlander and no character in fiction who remarked with fervour to his minister, "I really dinna ken ony greater pleasure on earth than a weel-gawin' law plea." Football was directly linked with war, for a football game had often cloaked an assembly of moss-troopers or cattle-raiders ; and if you want to test the Border spirit to-day, attend a Rugby football match between two of the teams that provide so many recruits for the Scottish side. Most Scottish games indeed —football, shinty, curling—and the Scottish ways of playing them, suggest far more a love of battle and a wish to keep warm than a respect for the team spirit.

A gentler legacy from Border fightings were the ballads that they inspired. Till far into the eighteenth century, each Border town had its piper, who in spring-time and after harvest toured a particular part of the country, singing the ballads and living on a small wage from the town, and presents in kind from his country hearers. There were also unlicensed wandering singers, and all through the century Border children grew up familiar with the deeds of Jamie Telfer of the Fair Dodhead, Dick o' the Cow, the Lads of Wamphray, with the Battle of Otterburn and Lesly's March ; and also with Young Tamlane and Clerk Saunders, Cospatrick and the Gay Goshawk. Medieval codes of chivalry, old tribal feuds, ancestral memories, pagan fears and dreads, belief in fairies, witches and brownies, in ghosts and spirits of dell and burn—all lived on in the romantic ballads and were a part of the Borderer's life. Nor did they strain with his religious beliefs ; the Reformation had reached the country late, and Borderers wore their Presbyterianism as easily as they once had their Catholicism.

This was the background to a great deal of Scott's life and writing; the life which Burns knew in Ayrshire and the West Country was very different. Here the living traditions were not of reckless freebooters, but of persecuted martyrs, the heroes were fanatic Covenanters, the old men in the chimney-corners would be better acquainted with Boston's *Fourfold State* than with the Ballad of Hardykanute. Over the country in general,

PITLESSIE FAIR
Detail from an oil painting by Sir David Wilkie, 1804

the rule of the Kirk was milder than in the religious wars of the seventeenth century. "Religion was just recovered," wrote Elizabeth Mure of her youth in the 1720's, "from the power of the Devil and fear of Hell, taught by our Mothers and Grandmothers." Ministers of the Moderate party went to the theatre, attended evening parties, and learnt whist to relieve the tedium of wet days in the country. But the older rule still held in many parishes of the West, and Burns was a regular victim of its severities. Several times he had to sit on the stool of repentance for getting girls into trouble : and the girls had to do the same penance. His friend and landlord,

21

THE VILLAGE WELL
Oil painting by Hugh Cameron, 1871

Gavin Hamilton, was summoned before the Kirk Session for slackness in attendance, and for sending a servant to dig up new potatoes on a Sunday. In retaliation, Burns pinned down the worst sides of Presbyterianism in his verses. In *The Holy Fair* he satirised the irreverence and drunkenness that might attend the open-air Communion, and in Holy Willie he pilloried the hypocritical Calvinist who, secure of his own salvation, contrived to commit the sins for which he brought others to book.

Yet however much he railed at it, Burns knew that the Kirk mattered, and in wider fields than the parochial. With its provincial synods as well as its National Assembly, the Kirk was the only organisation Scotland had left to her, and into its controversies and schisms went a great deal of the feeling that had no political outlet. And Burns too gives us the other side of the picture; in *The Cottar's Saturday Night* is all the homely piety he had known as a child, the Bible reading by the priestlike father, the family singing of the Metrical Psalms. And in Burns's own circumstances we see the light and dark of Scottish rural life. There is the squalid material background; the cottage at Alloway where he was born was better than most of its neighbours because it had a chimney, but the cattle lived under the same roof, and the midden smoked outside the door. There is the

22

THE BOWLERS
Detail from an oil painting by Sir George Harvey, 1850

desperately hard labour : when Burns was fourteen he was doing a man's work at the plough on a diet that seldom included meat. But then there is the passion for learning ; because there was no school near, Burns's father and six neighbours hired a schoolmaster at sixpence a day and his board, and by the age of seventeen Burns was reading Pope, Shakespeare, Locke and Addison. There is the easy intercourse between the classes—both Burns and Scott were able to move very freely up and down the social scale. Most of the lairds' sons still attended the village school, paying their fees in peats, meal and pence like the other lads ; and though their ways would diverge later, they would still meet on an easy footing. Not every ploughman or small farmer hobnobbed with lords, professors and county ladies as Burns did with Lord Glencairn, Dugald Stewart and Mrs. Dunlop of Dunlop ; but when a common interest happened to bring individuals from different backgrounds together, there was no difficulty in establishing a natural relationship, with dignity and independence respected on both sides.

Though the life of the community might be bleak and colourless, with no outlet for colour and pageantry, such as the Border towns had in their annual Ridings of the Marches, the songs which Burns did so much to preserve show the sweeter side of country life ; the people who sang

23

"Doun the burn, Davie" and "Whistle and I'll come to ye, my lad," were not quite borne down by hard work and poverty. And there were minor pleasures saved from an older order, Hallowe'en with its charms and spells, here and there old pagan fertility rites, celebrated on Beltane's Eve ; but the Kirk never came to terms with survivals from old religions, as did the Catholic Church in the Highlands and Islands. The shadow of its disapproval lay on these happenings, and even on the "penny weddings" when the friends of bride and bridegroom would contribute a feast in money and kind, and there would be dancing and junketing far into the night.

Calvinism took little account of the body ; and the body, left to itself, took its revenges. In these circumstances, it is not odd that drink should have filled so large a place in the life of Burns, and of Scotland in general. Alexander Carlyle, the minister of Inveresk, once complained that all John Bull cared about drink was "to go to bed muzzy" ; he may have been contrasting this with the fervour of the Scot, his wish to attain through drink an exaltation of spirit for which neither his religion nor his other activities provided a stimulus. This habit was certainly encouraged by the spread of whisky in the Lowlands, which at the beginning of the century had known nothing but ale ; and, with whisky at 1s. 8d. a quart and (in country districts) a public-house for every seventy of the population, it was an easy one to acquire. Burns shows us drink as fulfilling two main functions : in *John Barleycorn* and the *Epitaph on the Innkeeper of Mauchline* it opens the door to loftier regions—

> A dram was memento mori ;
> But a full-flowing bowl
> Was the saving his soul
> And port was celestial glory.

Elsewhere, drink is the sweetener of labour—

> oil'd by thee,
> The wheels o' life gae down-hill, scrievin'
> wi' rattlin' glee.

In 1707, Scotland threatened to become a poor little annexe to England, North Britain in fact ; by the end of the century she was a centre of economic, social and literary activity that drew the eyes of Europe. "Rules of taste in all the arts," said Voltaire, "from epic poems to gardening, come from Scotland." It was a remarkable revival, and its roots were in the soil. The really important event in the eighteenth century was not the '45, but the foundation, in 1723, of the Society of Improvers of Knowledge of Agriculture ; and high among the century's heroes stand Cockburn of Ormiston, introducing potatoes and turnips, Fletcher of Saltoun, experimenting with winnowing-fans, and the hundreds of forgotten lairds and farmers who by their interest in cattle-breeding, crop rotation, planting

By courtesy of the Fitzwilliam Museum, Cambridge

THE PENNY WEDDING

Water colour sketch by Sir David Wilkie, 1785-1841

HIGHLAND CHIEFS IN THE STEWART AND GORDON TARTANS
Coloured engraving after J. Logan by R. Havell, Junior, from Logan's *The Scottish Gael*, 1831

and scientific manuring, changed the face of Scotland and gave us the Cheviot sheep, the Clydesdale horse, the Ayrshire cow.

Life stirred too in other fields ; and the revival was all the more remarkable because it was not inspired by a unified national policy, a conscious national effort. It was mainly the doing of individuals, each working on his own line. There was Allan Ramsay the elder, providing a focus for Scottish letters in his wigmaker's shop in the High Street of Edinburgh, opening a circulating library, and printing the old Scotch songs. There was Allan Ramsay the younger, correspondent of Voltaire and Rousseau, painting the young wives and middle-aged intellectuals of Edinburgh with verve and delicacy. There was John Home showing, in his tragedy of *Douglas*, that there might be a Scottish theatre. There was David Hume writing *A Treatise on Human Nature* (1738) and Principal Robertson his *History of Scotland* (1759).

Gradually, these men and those they inspired, built up a society as lively and intelligent as any in Europe. Edinburgh once more became a focus. The rise in their rents enabled the country gentry to spend the winter in town ; students and learned men from all over Scotland, from England and from Europe, came to study under, or to argue with, Edinburgh's scholars and scientists. With material prosperity increasing, and the grimmer discipline of the Kirk relaxing, Scotsmen turned their energies to the arts of life.

For some years, the growing social life of Edinburgh struggled in the medieval setting of the Old Town where, because there was no room in the flats where people lived, all entertaining was done in taverns. The Englishman who had been attracted to Edinburgh by the reputation of her scholars would (like Colonel Mannering) be startled to find himself hobnobbing with these men renowned through half Europe in a dirty little den reached by a narrow close and a filthy outside staircase : but once arrived he would enjoy oysters—unusually plump and delicious oysters— claret and first-class talk. But after 1770 there was a setting worthy of the new society. In the streets, squares and crescents laid out by James Craig on the other side of the now drained Nor' Loch, life could have dignity and grace. Noblemen, law-lords, divines and professors could entertain in their own homes, and their guests could arrive in comfort in carriages, instead of in sedan chairs preceded by the ragged caddie who had been needed to show the way through the labyrinths of the Old Town.

To English visitors, one of the most pleasant features of this society was the position and charm of the women. They found the Scotch girls delightful to look at, their fresh complexions not coated over with paint, their walk free and active ; they were easy mixers, not oppressed by chaperones ; and lively talkers, for they were brought up with few inhibiting ideas of correct conversation. The stranger's approval was clinched when he found himself courteously and charmingly kissed on the cheek. The

25

THE OYSTER GIRL
Etching by John Kay, 1812

older ladies too were rewarding, if occasionally alarming also, dealing out racy anecdotes and salty repartees over their tea-tables and card-parties.

Those Scots who knew Europe best, such as Hume and Adam Smith, found Edinburgh a most congenial town to live in. Hume indeed, who had for years made Paris his home, could not make up his mind whether to settle there or in Edinburgh—never once did he consider London—but his final choice was of "retiring to Edinburgh and drinking my Claret" (at 18s. a dozen). Such good opinions of the city were confirmed by the visitors who arrived from England, Europe and America in increasing numbers, with letters of introduction to Hume and Adam Smith, Cullen the physician, Aiken the anatomist, Black the chemist (who weighed their curious gold pieces before he accepted them as students), Robertson the historian, Mackenzie the author of the *Man of Feeling*. They found themselves in a brilliant company that was still small enough to be homogeneous, where Hume hobnobbed with doctors of divinity, Adam Smith kept company

26

LORD CUNNINGHAM AND LORD GILLIES
Coloured engraving by Benjamin Crombie from his *Modern Athenians*, 1839

with novelists and poets, Monboddo the lawyer wrote on the origins of language. "Six weeks of the *densest* happiness I have ever met with in any part of my life" enthused Benjamin Franklin ; "Loaded with kindness" said the French geologist, Faujas de St. Fond, after his journey in 1784. Finer manners had not lessened the old Scottish pleasure in hospitality, and now that Scotch cooking was not inseparable from a dingy background, these strangers discovered a liking for haggis, broth and partan pie and cock-a-leekie.

Here then was Edinburgh in her golden age, one of the great cities of Europe, facing one way to London, one way to the Continent, ready to welcome travellers and ideas from both airts. This poise and self-confidence were based on particular achievements: they were not inspired by a strong national sentiment and self-assurance. David Hume put the problem to a friend : "Is it not strange that, at a time when we have lost our Princes, our Parliaments, our independent Government, even the Presence of our

27

chief Nobility, are unhappy, in our Accent and Pronunciation, speak a very corrupt Dialect of the Tongue which we make use of ; is it not strange, I say, that, in these Circumstances, we shou'd really be the People most distinguish'd for Literature in Europe ?" Here Hume touched on one of the oddest contradictions of the time. These Scots, who could hold their heads in any company in Europe, who looked down on London as far less civilised—were all terrified of writing anything but the purest Addisonian English. Talk in broad Scots they did, with vernacular idiom and accent ; but nothing of this must get into their prose. Hume compiled a list of Scotticisms so that his young countrymen should not spoil their chances of getting on in the wide world by saying "mind it" for "remember it," "marry upon" for "marry to," "butter and bread" for "bread and butter."

Pride in Hume, Black and the New Town there was in plenty ; pride in Scotch things as such, there was as yet little. But with the new century came a surge of national feeling, and the *élite* of Edinburgh realised that they were not only modern Athenians, citizens of the world, but heirs of a great and ancient nation. The chief author of this change was Walter Scott. In his poems and novels he made his countrymen conscious of being Scots ; he made them transcend the old boundaries and divisions, and interpreted Borderers to Highlanders, Covenanters to Episcopalians, Jacobites to Whigs, and made them all proud of being Scots, and proud of all their fellow-Scots. He roused this national feeling ; but it was not so much the dawn of a new renaissance as the magnificent sunset of an old world. He made Scots aware of their own language, their own manners, at a time when the language was being disowned and the manners anglicised. He immortalised them before they died ; he prolonged the life of many ; but he could not build up a new distinctively Scottish civilisation.

Yet under Scott's influence Scottish life had its great moments : and one of these was the visit to Edinburgh of George IV in 1824. Scott, prime organiser of the visit, appealed to Scotland's sense of the past. He hunted up Montrose's sword for the Knight Marshal to carry. He made full use of Edinburgh's historic buildings : the Castle, the Palace, Parliament House, St. Giles. He revived old customs and procedures, the bodyguard of Scottish Archers, the presentation of the keys of the city. He made Scotsmen see George, not as a foreign ruler, but as their rightful Scottish king, a descendant of the Stewarts. And Scotsmen rediscovered their own history. Once more the capital had a Sovereign and a Court—even though Holyrood was unfit for George to sleep in, and ceilings had to be propped up, and furniture borrowed, for the Levée and Drawing-room. Once more the Royal Mile deserved its name when the King, preceded by the Lord Lyon and the Mace, escorted by Highlanders and Greys, proceeded from Holyrood to the Castle through cheering crowds of citizens and visitors from all over the country. No such procession or pageantry had been seen since the old Riding of Parliaments.

WOMEN AT THE QUERN AND THE LUAGHAN WITH A VIEW OF TALYSKIR
Engraving from Pennant's *Tour in Scotland*, 1776

THE HIGHLANDS

"THE Hieland hills, the Hieland hills, I never see them but they gar me grew," groaned Bailie Nicol Jarvie as he advanced unwillingly into Rob Roy's country : and no wonder. The douce, commercial Glasgow he came from was a modern city ; now, stepping across the Highland Line, he was in some ways stepping into the middle ages. The wish that sent Dr. Johnson and the Lowland Boswell to visit the Hebrides in 1773 was to find "the circumstances of remote time," and "a system of life almost totally different from what we had been accustomed to see."

This Highland way of life was based on two main ideas : war, and the family. A Highland clan was essentially a large family, extending its arms to receive cousins of whatever degree of distance. The Chief might be judge and law-maker to his followers, but far more, he was their father, protector and provider. Everyday life expressed in a hundred ways this sense of the family. The clansman, however humble, had the same name as his chief ; wore the same tartan ; at feasts, sat at the same table. The chief regarded his foster-brothers with as much affection as his own, and illegitimate children were made welcome as members of this greater family.

There was every reason to welcome them, for in war, men are riches, and the clan was organised for war. Occasionally, as at Flodden, Highlanders fought for King and Scotland ; but in general they fought each other, sometimes for a blood-feud, sometimes for honour and prestige, but chiefly for land for better grazing, for a patch of arable soil. And when they could not get what they wanted within the Highlands, they turned to the Lowlands—fair game, to be plundered blithely without any offence to morality. Cattle were lifted, corn carried off, plunder brought in from as far afield as Ireland. In the early eighteenth century MacDonald of Keppoch's chief source of livelihood was cattle-raiding ; but some of his contemporaries got theirs by receiving blackmail from Lowlanders in return for protection and immunity.

Various adventurous visitors in the seventeenth and early eighteenth centuries, seeing the gaunt comfortless castle of the chief, and the chimneyless turf huts of his clansmen, the poor crops and the barelegged children, concluded that life in the Highlands was a miserable struggle for existence. It was a struggle, but not only a struggle ; and in many ways it was remarkably civilised. But with Highlanders, more than with most people, we must never confuse civilisation with comfort.

Chiefs who fought small wars against each other sent their sons to the universities : indeed Donald, Lord of the Isles, who challenged the King of Scots at the battle of Harlaw in 1411, had been at Oxford. MacDonald of Barrisdale, a great levyer of blackmail, was also a scholar, with two lines of Virgil engraved on his broad sword. The lesser clansmen might not have many chances of polite education, but they had a living culture. The sagas of Deirdre and Cuchullin, Finn MacCoul and Oisin, all that great body of legend that Scotland shares with Ireland, were a part of their existence, and they were continually being re-told in new forms and metres of great beauty and complexity. As well as holding the old sagas in his head, and the history of the clan, and a ten-centuries' genealogy of the chief, a bard had to be able to make new songs and sagas out of contemporary events. He was an important craftsman : so too was the piper, who had possibly spent some years at the college of piping in Skye, or in Mull. Dances and marches he played, of course, but his great achievement was the classical composition in several movements, the pibroch ; the scope of this complex art must not be judged by the occasional begging pipers heard in the streets of Edinburgh or London, nor even by the best military pipe-band.

Sagas and pibrochs might be for great occasions ; but everyday life was sweetened by dancing, singing and poetry. There were the *ceilidhs*, or evening gatherings in the cottages, for songs and stories while the girls knitted, the boys busked their fishing hooks, and peeled willow-wands for baskets. The harvesters sang in time to the strokes of the sickle; the boatmen sang at their oars in the chief's galley; the women sang as they worked the cloth, one singing the verse, the others joining in the chorus ; the

30

HIGHLANDER
Chalk drawing by Sir David Wilkie, 1785-1841

islesmen sang as they gathered the seaweed. These songs were not just the expression of happiness—often, indeed, the subject of the songs was sad—they were a necessary part of the action ; but they probably contributed to happiness by giving the action a rhythm, raising a dull task above the level of drudgery, and giving each worker a sense of community with the others. The more solitary occupations had their songs too ; a girl sang to her cows up in the summer sheilings on the mountains, the shoemaker as he counted his tools ; there were songs for going a journey, for healing a toothache, for every landmark in the four seasons, for every occasion of a person's life, from his birth and baptism to his death and burying. For in the Highlands, religion had come to terms with the old beliefs, and there was a harmonious connection between men's work, play, hopes, fears, beliefs and dreams. Nor had the Reformation made much difference, for Catholic and Protestant wore their faith easily and were tolerant of each other.

This life could continue as long as the Highlands were difficult to reach ; and the first great attack on it came from General Wade the roadmaker, between the Risings of the 'fifteen and the 'forty-five. He pushed his roads up the Garry and down the Spey, into Badenoch and Lochaber, and over the 2,500 feet of the Corrieyairack Pass, so that soldiers could be marched quickly from one fort to another. But the roads brought traders too, from Glasgow and Leith, who began to think of dealing in Highland salmon, herring and whisky ; with another, and in many ways higher standard of life displayed to them, the Highlanders no longer enjoyed that isolation in which their society had grown and flourished. The drovers who kept to the old grassy tracks, the clansmen who tried to destroy the new roads, were realising, however obscurely, the seriousness of the challenge. Then came the '45, and showed the clan structure still standing, with clansmen following Prince Charlie, or holding back, according to the choice of their chief : and then came the consequences of the '45, and shattered it. After the Rising, the Highlander's life had lost its mainspring. His chief might be in exile, his lands and powers taken from him ; his claymore and gun might be in the hands of the Government (or in his own thatch, or buried in the bog) ; his target now served as the lid of his butter-milk barrel ; with the tartan banned, he himself worked his fields in unfamiliar clothes. If he was one who had earned his keep in the clan by fighting, he might have no fields to work. And so he began to turn his eyes beyond the Highlands, to Georgia, the Carolinas, to his own Lowlands. Indeed, there had been emigration before the '45 ; the Highlands had never been able entirely to support their population with its large numbers of non-productive fighting-men, and as the central government made it more difficult to replenish the larder the traditional way, by raiding the Lowlands, the only chance for many was to go abroad. The French wars provided alternative occupation in plenty : between 1793 and 1815 forty battalion of line and seven of militia, 37,600 men, were raised in the

32

FLORA MACDONALD

Oil painting by Allan Ramsay, c. 1749

By courtesy of the Trustees of the Tate Gallery

THE EMIGRANTS

Oil painting by William McTaggart, 1891

Highlands. Skye alone, in the first half of the nineteenth century, raised 10,000 soldiers, including 21 generals. And the new regiments, being based on the clans, preserved much of the old family feeling, which the Government encouraged by giving the chiefs command of battalions, and making them an allowance for each clansman who followed them to the colours.

And yet in some parts the old order showed itself surprisingly resilient to the first attacks. Elizabeth Grant has left us a picture of Rothiemurchus between 1800 and 1830 which shows how much of the old life remained. Her father, the seventh laird, was the chief and father of his country. He commanded the local volunteers, and all his officers were Macphersons or Grants, tenants of little farms in Strathspey or Badenoch. His own house at the Doune was barely-furnished, but full of relatives and retainers, including a piper who refused all work unconnected with whisky for fear of spoiling the delicacy of his touch. As half the people in the district were called Grant, the tenants were known by the name of their lands, Ballindalloch, Tullochgorm, Kinchurdy, and others by the work they did, like Jenny Dairy. (Both these habits persist in the Highlands to-day, and in a village over the hills from Rothiemurchus letters are delivered by Maggie Postie, while the taxidermist who deals with the stags' heads for the shooting tenant is Jockie Stuffer.)

There was a strong feeling for any member of the family ; when Elizabeth Grant was taken on a visit to Inverness and Forres, she and her mother spent their time calling on Grant after Grant—dressmakers, schoolmistresses, a Provost's wife, a retired Colonel, a laird's lady—but all of the clan. There was the old kindly attitude to illegitimates, and most households had one of these "accidental children," no mystery being made of their birth, no shame attaching to them, and the family all anxious to see them make their way and marry well. The hospitality was tremendous. The doors were never locked and visitors poured in during the summer and autumn—"no one then ever passed a friend's house in the Highlands, nor was it ever thought necessary to send invitations on the one part, or to give information on the other." No barefoot boy with a message from the gamekeeper or forester went empty away; whisky, oatcake and cheese were given to all comers. The Laird's lady, handing the horn cup to a woodman's wife, was startled to see her, after taking a good pull, pass it on to the wee thing trotting beside. "My goodness, child" said Lady Grant, "doesn't it *bite* you ?" "Ay, but I like the bite," replied the creature.

At weddings, there was dancing ; at a death, a respectful visit to the corpse, with refreshments provided, and later a funeral feast. Then every season had its diversions. In winter, Hogmanay, and the holiday for all who worked in the forest—with shinty by day (fifty a side), dinner in the barns, and dancing at night, with two sets of fiddlers playing, punch made in the washing-tubs, and the lads kissing the girls as they set them in their places for reel or strathspey. In autumn were the harvest homes, and the

33

Pitmain Tryst—with cattle-dealing in the morning, a great dinner for drovers, farmers and lairds, and a ball in the evening for everybody. At all these gatherings, family feeling was strong and class feeling almost absent. The houses of the great lairds were so far apart, and travel so difficult that the people of the "big house" joined wholeheartedly in the social life going on all round them instead of confining themselves to the company of other grandees.

The sad comment on this busy lively life in Rothiemurchus is that the laird went bankrupt ; even though he, luckier than many Highlanders, had the great Rothiemurchus forests to bring in a considerable money income. The bitter truth was that few chieftains could hope to keep up their old open-handed style unless they drew some income from outside the Highlands. A few turned their energies wholly towards improving their estates, but many more tried to meet their own needs by ways which helped to weaken what remained of the clan structure. They found, as Rothiemurchus did, "a new and profitable scheme for making money out of the bare moors in the Highlands" by letting their hills for shooting. And they found that they could collect more rent by renting their hill-pastures to sheep-farmers from the Lowlands, than by leaving them in the hands of a number of small tenants.

This is not the place to go into the heartrending story of how the cottagers were turned out of their glens and driven to emigrate as the only hope ; but no one can understand the Highlands unless he feels something of the sadness that hangs over the empty hills and glens, the deserted sheilings and ruined cottages. Quite possibly it was to the ultimate advantage of many a Highlander that he went abroad. "It is just possible," wrote Alexander Smith as he watched a boat-load of emigrants off Skeabost in Skye, "that what is for the landlord's interest may be for yours also in the long run ; but you feel that the landlord has looked after his own interest in the first place."

This indeed was the heart of the matter. The chief who had been the father of his people was now the man of business ; once the welfare of his whole clan had decided his actions, now he acted with an eye to his bank balance. Money had played a small part in the old days when there was little of it ; a chief's importance had been measured by the length not of his purse, but of his tail of followers ; a girl's dowry had been given in cows, rent paid in kind, and relationships within the clan had not been on a cash basis. Now many of the former chiefs accepted the new standard only too wholeheartedly and part of the pathos of the emigrants' laments, "Lochaber No More," "I'll Never, I'll Never, I'll Never Return," comes from this sense that old ties once held sacred had been brutally snapped.

The spectacular attacks on Highland life had come mainly after the '45, but for nearly two hundred years before one of its main components, the Gaelic, had been steadily undermined. Governments identified it with

34

ST. FILLAN'S GAMES
Engraving from Wilson's *Scotland Illustrated*, 1845

sedition and Jacobitism; the Kirk, with popery, and relics of heathen superstition; between them, they made it almost impossible for any child to get any education in its native tongue. Gaelic remained the language of love songs, of working songs, of family life: English, the language of reason, learning, and getting on in the world. Gaelic had been an integral part of the Highlander's whole culture; but when the schoolmaster, the minister, and the world in general represented it as something that held him back, it was no wonder if often he lost confidence not only in his language but in the life it belonged to.

Later, the Kirk withdrew its opposition, seeing the advantages of doing missionary work in a language the natives understood, and if you go to church to-day in Mull or Skye, you will find services in Gaelic; but

35

the districts and islands where the old songs and music still flourish most are those, like the Island of Barra, which never knew the Reformation. Alexander Carmichael, the great collector of Gaelic songs, was baptised and buried a Presbyterian ; but when he revisited Lewis in the eighteen-eighties, he was saddened to find the old music and singing killed by the Kirk, and the islanders taught to distrust it as folly. For one of the misfortunes of the Highlands was that they received, in the nineteenth century, a dose of fundamentalist Calvinism, after the rest of the country had more or less won free from it. To match the religious excesses and scruples of the Covenanting Johnston of Warriston to-day, we have to go to the far North, perhaps to the town whose Provost was excommunicated from the Free Church for merely looking on at a dance. But we must never generalise too much about the Highlands, and against these pictures of the Kirk as a kill-joy must be set such another as Norman Macleod drew of Morven in the nineteenth century—the gaiety in the Manse, with fiddling, dancing, and story-telling, the deep beauty of a Communion Sunday with boats crossing the Sound bringing people from twenty or thirty miles away to sing psalms and receive the sacrament on the greensward.

Life in the Highlands is a favourite subject for sentimentalists, but there must have been something remarkably tough in it : looking back over the last hundred years, and remembering all these attacks on livelihood, customs and language, we are surprised not that so much has been lost, as that anything has been saved. Those years have indeed increased the loss. The tide of emigration did not slacken, but it became more selective ; fewer whole families embarked, the young people went and the old stayed at home. Mountain ranges, long arms of the sea and stormy straits still cut off one community from another, and as conditions have improved elsewhere in the country, the Highlander has felt himself increasingly handicapped in his effort to make a living. Transport has been good enough to bring gym tunics to schoolgirls in Skye, or Glasgow bread and bakeries to crofts which once lived on their own scones and oatcakes; but people in Moidart have had to pay 25s. a ton to get their goods brought by boat from Mallaig. Life has still depended on wealth coming from outside—from the money sent by sons in Canada or New Zealand, or daughters in service in Glasgow or London ; from the rents from deer-forest and shooting-lodge paid by the enterprising American or the ambitious stockbroker.

The links between the great Highland landlords and the upper class in England have been strengthened, at the expense of those with their own people ; and even those who made their homes in the Highlands would probably send their sons to English public schools and universities. ("Sir," said Dr. Johnson after talking with the Eton-bred Sir Alexander Macdonald of Armadale, "the Highland chiefs should not be allowed to go farther south than Aberdeen"). The Highland social life of pre-war summers, so

GROUSE SHOOTING BY THE SOUTHERNER
Engraving by Hunt from a painting by F. C. Turner, 1841

fully recorded in *The Times*, and copiously illustrated in *The Tatler*, was in the main the life of one class only. True, a few of those who tossed the caber and threw the hammer at the Games at Portree and Inverness might be descendants of clansmen who had found these sports a training for war. But the faces at the Highland Balls are not very different from those seen at the Fourth of June at Eton, or at Commemoration at Oxford. With their tartans and reels these delightful balls are livelier than dances in the South ; but to the majority who attend them, however kilted, the Highlands are essentially a holiday place, and not the scene of their whole life and work.

Yet still, numbers of Highlanders venerate their chief, though bound to him now by sentiment only, and no longer common interest. Long after the Duke of Argyll had bought Iona, the islanders considered themselves the people of Maclean. The late Marquis of Huntly lost all his Deeside estates and spent the summer in a villa in Aboyne, but he was still Cock of the North. Since the first disarming, the chiefs have had a gradually diminishing field in which to exercise their powers ; for many, now, it has been narrowed down to pride in status only. The man whose ancestors had the right of pit and gallows may be touchy about being given his rank and precedence,

37

fussy about being addressed by his right title. When Johnson published his *Journey to the Western Islands* he got into trouble for saying that Macleod of Raasay acknowledged the chieftainship of Macleod of Skye, and publicly apologised in the Edinburgh newpapers. Not long before this war, large sums of money were spent in the Court of Session to establish who was the rightful holder of a title which carried no land, no Lord, no Sir, but beside which any knight or baron would look shabby in Highland eyes.

Clan feeling has persisted, especially in the antagonism of most of the Highlands to the Campbells, who still have to pay in hostility and suspicion for the support their ancestors gave the Government two and three hundred years ago. No Stewart from Appin would be best pleased at hearing that his daughter wished to marry a Campbell. Sadder testimonies to the strength of clan ties are the 1914-1918 war memorials all over the Highlands ; at Ullapool, in Wester Ross, more than half the names are Mackenzies, serving in the Seaforth Highlanders. Memories are still long, and the events of three centuries ago still near and familiar. In Appin, The Murder is still the shooting of Colin Campbell in 1752 (the story of *Kidnapped*) ; in Glencoe, the Massacre is spoken of with a living sorrow.

In everyday life there are still traces of the old pattern. In the black house in the Outer Hebrides there are still songs, in Gaelic, round the peat fire at night. The Highlander is still hospitable, and will not easily turn anyone from his door. Determined to get full value for their sporting rights, some landlords, like the late owner of Rhum, have forbidden their tenants, on threat of eviction, to take in visitors in case they should disturb the sport ; nothing has caused greater anger than this violation of a deep-seated instinct.)

The Highlander is still slow to think of a relationship in purely money terms; still slow to value material comfort. To the brisk outsider he often looks lazy; and by southern standards he may be lazy; but this is partly the result of a climate where the prevailing south-west wind always brings rain, where by November the corn may still be too sodden to harvest, and the potatoes too wet to lift. In Canada and New Zealand the Highland emigrant has not been accused of sloth.

But this attitude is also an assertion of old beliefs : that life is not all work, that an afternoon's conversation may be more agreeable than an extra one-and-sixpence, that even a small plumbing job is worthy of a ceremonial approach, with cups of tea and polite intercourse, that it is more important to pay respect to your dead neighbour by shutting your shop for two days than to turn your stock over quickly. Life in the glens and islands to-day is often hard and sometimes squalid, the framework of the old ways has collapsed and no new one has been built, these traces we cherish are only traces, a shadow of a lost substance, but as long as those values are asserted at all, the whole community is the richer for the Highland way of life.

GOLF COURSE IN ALEXANDRA PARK, GLASGOW
Etching by G. Aikman after John Smart

TO THE PRESENT DAY

IN the eighteenth century Scotland recovered from destitution; in the nineteenth, she became rich (by the standard of other countries of her size, if not of England), discovering the wealth hidden in her coal-fields, her rivers, and in the engineering skill of her people. With the increase of wealth came an increasing regard for wealth, in terms of bank balances and share certificates, and money differences began to play a larger part in separating one group from another. Towns that had been compact and neighbourly, developed West Ends; people whose fathers had lived side by side developed different codes in eating and speech. Glasgow was the capital of the new prosperity, and in Glasgow the difference was most marked. The minority who earned and pocketed the wealth hived off to comfortable villas in Hillhead and Kelvinside, the majority who only earned it swarmed in the gloomy great tenements, "the colour of mud, built to last for ever, cut up into boxes, with a tap on the staircase." And when we talk about how the Scots lived last century, we have to remember that half the population lived in one or two-roomed houses.

Glasgow, which had been a charming modest clean town, run by a Town Council guided by the Kirk Session, became an industrial giant so quickly that it broke out of the habitual mould of its life. There was no time for gradual development, new patterns had to be made, both in tenement and West End. The latter had no resident aristocracy to set the tone; and the social life it worked out for itself was a vigorous and independent growth. The men who mastered seas, winds and metals, commanded

39

the material world to serve them in their own homes too. In the house of a Glasgow merchant or shipbuilder in the 'sixties and 'seventies material comfort—and warm-hearted hospitality—stood at a very high level : as many maids as were needed to tend the numerous coal fires, dust the ornaments and carry the gleaming brass water cans, and ten to twelve courses as a regular standard for a dinner party. The wealth sometimes burst out grandly—as when Glasgow shipbuilders (under the formidable eye of the picture-dealer Reid) bought Boudins, Sisleys and Manets while their Merseyside contemporaries were still putting their money on the Royal Academy; or showily as when they bought yachts in which they really did enjoy and explore the incomparable West Highland coast. But in the main it went into a high standard of material living, of which the Clyde hydropathic is one fitting symbol ; and another the Glasgow tea-shop, invention of the great Miss Cranston, with its spread of bakeries so astonishing to the visiting English, to whom tea-shop meant only the marble-topped tables of their London A.B.C.'s. Miss Cranston herself had C. R. Mackintosh, the architect so appreciated by Europe, to design the furniture and plate in her tea-rooms ; the arts played a living if limited part in Glasgow life.

In the back streets, however, the struggle to live at all was fierce, and till a decent water supply was brought from Loch Katrine in the 'sixties, typhus regularly swept off its quota. Yet these tenement kitchens and narrow closes produced a life not quite like that of any other big industrial city. It was not behind the West End in hospitality, and far beyond it in neighbourliness, with one person's luck or sorrow shared by all the other families in the building. It was centred on the new shipyards, but it was shot through with old ways of thought—with the fervour and particularity of Covenanters debating Election by Grace, the orators on Glasgow Green differentiated between socialism and syndicalism. Its presiding deity was the Clyde, symbolising both work and release—work in the yards and release in the annual outing "doon the wa'er" ; its ideal of beauty, the lines of a windjammer, or the new Cunarder down at John Brown's yard ; its criterion of excellence, "Clyde built."

Nor was this life entirely uprooted from the country. Glasgow had largely drawn its workers from the Highlands, but it did not totally absorb them. Boys who from windows four stories up could see the blue hills of Arran would not quickly forget their own blue hills of Ross or Appin ; on Friday evenings there would be groups waiting for the Oban *Times* or the *Ross-shire Journal* to find who had won the ploughing match, and how the row over the new manse was going ; annually Arran natives, men of Skye and Lochfyneside exiles, would troop to the Waterloo Rooms for a Soirée, Concert and Ball. In this were mild echoes of the clans ; but one division in Glasgow life touched deeper conflicts. The Irish had begun to arrive early in the century, the hungry 'forties drove them across in armies,

40

By courtesy of the Artist and Messrs. Colnaghi, London

THE KIRK, ISLE OF WHITHORN, WIGTOWNSHIRE

Water colour by Sir Muirhead Bone

THE CLYDE FROM PORT GLASGOW

Oil painting by Stanley Spencer

and by 1851 every sixth person in Glasgow was Irish. Religion was one cause of discord between them and the Scots ; another was their backwardness in joining trades unions. They brought their own spites with them, and their Green-Orange rows set the tone for the larger Scottish-Irish engagement. Rational and irrational feelings centred on this issue ; the crowd at the Rangers v. Celtic match are fanatics in other things than football. ("Rangers 3, Celtic o. Aye, there'll be sair herts in the Vatican the nicht !") The game sublimates some of the passion which the Irish question has generated, but not all—much went into the knife-slashing gang fights that have troubled Glasgow in our own days. Zest and fierceness have been marks of Glasgow life—the robustious Christmas Pantomime and the political radicalism of the Clyde are both expressions of this spirit. Nor was it killed by the appalling living conditions of most of Glasgow's inhabitants, nor by the empty years when through no fault of their own skilled hands lay idle and nothing but the dole came in. And when the Glasgow worker drank he could do it like Burns, not only to forget his circumstances, but to rise above them. "I belong tae Glesca," begins the ditty—

"But when I get tight on a Saturday night
Glesca belongs tae me."

But Glasgow was not all extremes of wealth or poverty, and at the firm core of the city were the great number of foremen, warehousemen, draughtsmen, clerks and shopkeepers, who sent their sons and daughters into the professions, supported the Scottish Orchestra and the Art Union, and who lived rather less stereotyped lives than their opposite numbers in English manufacturing towns. It was the men of this breed that Stefansson preferred for his self-supporting Arctic expeditions.

No other town changed character as drastically as Glasgow. In Aberdeen, new industries brought new wealth, and the city pushed out a spacious granite West End, but it remained firmly based on a rich countryside. (For its baron of beef at the Lord Mayor's banquet, the City of London has to come to Aberdeen). On market days, the farmers fill the solid eating-houses, the lairds the Club in Union Street, and the whole town takes on a country air. With several centuries of independent action behind them—Aberdeen had taken the unpopular side in the seventeenth-century religious wars, had contentedly kept bishops when the rest of Scotland was cursing them—Aberdonians calmly took their tone from no-one but themselves. Not so immediately hospitable as Glasgow, not so touchy socially as Edinburgh, Aberdeen remained a self-confident compact community, more interested in what was happening on its doorstep, or at the ends of the earth, than in the events of the rest of Scotland. (Two headlines, they used to say, were kept in permanent type in the old *Aberdeen Free Press* : "Eminent Aberdonian Honoured Abroad," ran one ; and the other "Theft of a Washing-Tub at Inverurie.") Aberdeen's self-assurance is reflected in

41

its building : early in the nineteenth century the Town Council thought it worth while to go bankrupt over making a decent main street, which for half its length had to be expensively carried far above the natural level of the ground: and of all Scottish cities, it has the most seemly new suburbs.

Glasgow, in the prime of her industrial vigour, could afford to scoff at Edinburgh's slower, traditional ways. But Edinburgh's great days were already over. There was no group of men to compare with those of the Golden Age. Some of her publishers had moved to London, and so had the *Edinburgh Review* ; the city was no longer a place of pilgrimage for intellectual Europe. "Half a capital, half a country town," Stevenson called her in the 'seventies, but the capital side was rather shabby. Edinburgh still had the Law of Scotland, and the Churches flocked to her every summer for their General Assemblies as they still do. Then for a fortnight ministers and elders from the Shetlands and Galloway, Caithness and Kintyre, would meet old cronies, attend the Moderator's ample breakfasts, debate the affairs of their Church, and have the sense of belonging to a truly national community. Then too the Lord High Commissioner would drive up to the Assembly of the Church of Scotland from Holyrood, where he stayed in state as the King's representative, "a kind of stage sovereign, among stage courtiers." But for the rest of the year the Palace, like Edinburgh's other historic places, was shown to tourists, and looked only to the past ; present history was made elsewhere.

Gone was the cheerful hugger-mugger of the old life in the high *lands* where all classes mixed with easy familiarity. Edinburgh society sorted itself out carefully with the Law, the University, the Church, the doctors, forming an intricate pattern of cliques and hierarchies. Even the rebels were affected : Stevenson (as John Buchan observed) could never have come from Glasgow or Aberdeen : his modish Bohemianism was simply Edinburgh gentility upended.

Yet though money made new splits and divisions, it was still comparatively easy for Scots to move up through the classes. Education was the great ladder, for it remained as true as in Scott's time that "a certain portion of learning is easily attained by those who are willing to suffer hunger and thirst in exchange for acquiring Greek and Latin." (For its size, Scotland has twice as many University students as England). For most of the nineteenth century the session was from October to May, so that a student might help on the farm at home or otherwise earn his living for nearly half the year. It was the normal thing for the clever lad from the village school to proceed to the University: a man who lived in a black house in the Isles might have a son a Professor at Aberdeen, the father of an Edinburgh surgeon would be a crofter on Speyside, and such situations would be the cause of pride, but not at all of surprise.

There were local rivalries between the four Universities, but there were no poor relations, no gulf of social prestige to mark some off from others

THE FISHER'S LANDING
Oil painting by William McTaggart, 1877

as there is between Oxford and Cambridge and the rest of the English universities. The professors of the last century formed perhaps the most fortunate class in the country. They enjoyed the prestige that Scots give to those concerned with education. They had contact with the academic world beyond Scotland, and they were not oppressed by Presbyterianism in its more rigid and gloomy aspects. In St. Andrews and Aberdeen, they lived in surroundings of great beauty and dignity. Their children went to the local Academy or High School, to receive a sound education at small cost and the opportunity to work with boys and girls from every kind of home. They had long holidays—under the old dispensation which still holds good for some chairs, from May to October—and, whatever their University, they had, within five shillings' railway fare or less, some of the best country in Scotland. On their moderate salaries, they brought up large families of children, who enjoyed a free, lively, and fairly cultured life, who got up plays and societies, spent summer months in Arran or Deeside, and in whose ears those horrifying stories of the dreary Scottish Sabbath sound like something in a book.

"The eighteenth was the final Scotch century"; we may dispute this judgment of Lord Cockburn, made in 1847, and yet recognise with him the inroads made by anglicisation on the distinctively Scottish way of life. "Scarcely a single Scotch nobleman will keep a house in a single Scotch

43

town," was one of his chief complaints. Those of the upper classes who spent most of the year in the South might, on their summer visits to their Scottish country-houses, resume part of the old pattern ; wear the kilt, address their neighbours by the name of their properties, attend the agricultural show, judge the piping at the local Games. Indeed they—or their English sporting tenants—might observe these occasions far more thoroughly than the people who lived in the district all the year round ; but they would not hold the same degree of responsibility for the parish school, the new manse, the proposed drainage plan. Yet when they went South again in the autumn, the local gentry would be left feeling slightly stranded and provincial ; and throughout the nineteenth century the standard set by the class to which Scotland was mainly a place of occasional residence became in many points the ideal for the socially ambitious Scot. Gradually, two distinct patterns emerged for the well-to-do. The main features of the first were the public school, Oxford or Cambridge, the Episcopalian church, an English accent. And to those who aspired to this pattern, the characteristics of the other—High School or Academy, Scottish University, the Presbyterian Church, a recognisable Scottish tongue—were signs of a less gentle breeding. (Scottish Episcopalianism is in some districts of old and honourable ancestry ; but when you hear a Presbyterian snorting about Piskies, the chances are that he will be thinking of some wealthy business-man who, having bought an estate and set up as a laird, is persuaded by his wife to line up with the rest of the county and attend the Episcopal Church).

Of course there were, and are, all sorts of combinations between the two patterns. There might be Etonians with a Scotch accent, Episcopalians at George Watson's ; many of the Scottish gentry, after their years of education in England, have settled to a lifetime of useful work on county council, agricultural society, and Kirk Session. And the fact that the Royal Family, when at Holyrood or Balmoral, attends the Church of Scotland, has delicately complicated the social situation. But over a long period there have been more conversions from the second pattern to the first than from the first to the second.

So for the most lively manifestations of Scottish manners in the last century and this, we must go beyond the upper class and the wealthy to circles which regard an "English accent" as slightly comic, observe Hogmanay, and which every 25th of January toast the Immortal Memory. For Burns, who suffered from a religion which made few concessions to mens' need for symbolism and ceremonial, has inspired what is almost the religion of the Burns Nichts. His poetry may not always be much in evidence on these occasions, but the memory of what he was as a man—with his drink, his girls, his love of Scotland, his belief in the brotherhood of man —and the celebration of it in haggis and whisky, provide for thousands of his countrymen the satisfaction and release of a lofty ritual.

44

FISHING SEASON, STORNOWAY
Pen drawing by Sir Muirhead Bone

The Kirk has been still the distinctive Scottish institution : the foundation of the Free Church in 1843 may be read as a refusal to let outsiders tamper with this last stronghold. 1843 was the occasion of a great release of social energy : the laymen and ministers who built new churches in almost every parish, built more than churches. They built centres of corporate life, church societies based not so much on restrictions and prohibitions as on creative activities. If in Burns's day the social life of the Kirk meant sitting in penance on a cutty-stool, a century later the typical picture was the foreign missions bazaar. Such occasions can be easily mocked : but in Bible classes, sewing meetings, literary societies and missionary activities, the Free Church—and, following suit, the Auld Kirk —was giving a focus to social energies, and cultivating a sense of common responsibilities, such as no other institution but the trades unions could provide.

As we come towards our own day, local idiosyncracies and quiddities there are in plenty : Newhaven fishwives still, on special occasions, wear their striped petticoats, the Border towns still hold their summer festivals of the Braw Lads Gathering and the Common Ridings, farm-hands in Aberdeenshire still sing their bothy ballads, and the Buchan dialect is still an impenetrable mystery to those who live south of the Dee. But are these just local survivals and variations of a norm, such as we find in any part remote from a nation's capital—indeed, is Scotland but the largest and remotest of English counties? Or is there still a distinctive and valuable Scottish way of life that can still produce new manifestations ?

45

In 1935 or so, many might have doubted this. They would admit a few signs of native vitality : the astonishing growth of amateur drama (but this movement affected England also) ; the more frequent Royal visits to Holyrood which gave Edinburgh days of intensive and coloured activity ; the transfer of most of the Scottish Office from London to Edinburgh ; the reappearance, in Scots writing, of the coarse rough fibre that marked Scots literature in the great days of the makars ; the revival, with gusto, of reels and the more vigorous country dances; the increased number of kilts in Princes Street ; the B.B.C.'s start in broadcasting Gaelic. But, having admitted so much, they would brush all these things aside as of minor importance beside the formidable factors that pulled the other way : the wireless programmes that were not Scots or Gaelic ; the transport that could bring Lyons' cakes and American advertisements to the farthest corners, the continued drift away, to England and overseas ; more than all, the dreadful levelling agency of the depression (and in the worst years the Scottish unemployed, with their dependants, formed nearly a third of the total population). Life on the dole is not so different in the Gorbals or Jarrow ; there is a limit to the national variations that can be played on bread, tea and margarine, and the queues at the Labour Exchange.

And yet, those who doubted in 1935 might ten years later have thought afresh. No-one who was in Scotland in 1940, when the loss of the 51st Division at St. Valéry struck the country as another Flodden, is likely to underrate what Scotland has lost in this war. And that was only the first blow. But, released by the necessities of war, tides of new life swept into Scotland. Into glens which had once sent their sons to Canada came great companies of Canadian lumbermen-soldiers. The village halls which in winter months had housed a few whist-drives, socials and lantern-lectures, now had dances twice a week : and in their log-built camps the visitors demonstrated that electric light and water can be brought to small Highland settlements without heavy outlay in installations. The Clyde was once more a river of life, with every yard working, every tide bringing in food, men and help, and the *Queen Mary* and *Queen Elizabeth* visible to all, crossing the oceans without escort, running to schedule like clockwork, U-boats or no U-boats—and bonny ships, Clyde-built! At Prestwick in Ayrshire, now become the greatest airport in the kingdom, generals and ambassadors arrived from Washington, leaders of the United Nations emplaned for America. History was being made in Scotland now, and Scots no longer suffered from the curse of the provincial, the feeling that life is going on elsewhere, and has left him high and dry.

This confidence was reflected in domestic matters. In Glasgow was born a theatre where new Scottish plays have been successfully—and profitably—produced without the management cocking an eye to London as ultimate arbiter of what the theatre can do. The Saltire Society, founded not long before the war to encourage Scottish culture, increased in member-

46

THE BLACK WATCH LANDING IN SICILY
Water colour by I. G. N. Eadie, 1944

ship, standing and effectiveness ; by its vigorous discussions, publications and inquiries, by its direct action in matters affecting Scotland's looks and housing, it made its members not only custodians of a past culture, but creators of a present.

Possibly the most enduring influence of the war was the arrival of the Poles, the Czechs and the Norwegians who found a home in Scotland in these years. Except in painting, where the links with Paris had always been strong, Scotland had too often been meeting Europe at second-hand. Occasionally the Gifford Lectures would bring a Barth or a Gilson direct to Edinburgh or Aberdeen, but to most foreigners Scotland was a distant (if interesting) part of Britain that might be tacked on to a London-based visit if time allowed. Now these allies from Europe were brought face to face with Scotland, and Scotland rose to the occasion. Old links with Norway and Poland were remembered, and made the basis of a new alliance. When these strangers praised her tartans and her music, the Scot's own pride in them was renewed. Deeper than such occasional manifestations went a sense of sympathy with these other nations. Each of them had a culture and a way of life it thought worth fighting for: Scotland, comparable to them in size and wealth, as well as in old traditions of hard-won independence, realised afresh that the life and ways of wealthier England were

47

not the only possible criterion. Their presence in Scotland and the links then formed gave Scotland new dignity, conscious once more of her place in Europe ; and gave her too new confidence in her capacity to live a life and nourish a culture that should be not merely North British, but positively and worthily Scots.

SATURDAY BARROWS NEAR ALBERT BRIDGE, GLASGOW
Detail from a drawing by Sir Muirhead Bone, 1910

SHORT BIBLIOGRAPHY

Early Travellers in Scotland by P. Hume Brown.—*Domestic Life in Scotland 1488-1688* by John Warrack.—*Scottish Diaries and Memoirs 1550-1746*, and *1746-1843* by J. G. Fyfe.—*Social and Economic Development of Scotland before 1603* and *Everyday Life in Old Scotland* by I. F. Grant.—*Social Life in Scotland since 1707* by George S. Pryde.—*Social Life in Scotland in the Eighteenth Century* by H. G. Graham.—*Autobiography* by Alexander Carlyle.—*A Journey to the Western Islands* by Samuel Johnson.—*Memoirs of a Highland Lady* by Elizabeth Grant.—*Reminiscences of a Highland Parish* by Norman Macleod.—*Memorials of his Time 1779-1850* by Lord Cockburn.—*From One Century to Another* by E. S. Haldane.